Animal Homes

Foxes and Their Dens

by Martha E. H. Rustad

Consulting Editor: Gail Saunders-Smith, PhD

Consultant: William John Ripple, Professor
Oregon State University
Corvallis, Oregon

Capstone
press

Mankato, Minnesota

Pebble Plus is published by Capstone Press
151 Good Counsel Drive, P.O. Box 669, Mankato, Minnesota 56002
www.capstonepress.com

1 2 3 4 5 6 09 08 07 06 05 04

Library of Congress Cataloging-in-Publication Data
Rustad, Martha E. H. (Martha Elizabeth Hillman), 1975–
    Foxes and their dens / by Martha E. H. Rustad.
    p. cm.—(Pebble plus: Animal homes)
    Includes bibliographical references (p. 23) and index.
    ISBN 0-7368-2583-5 (hardcover)
    1. Foxes—Habitations—Juvenile literature. [1. Foxes—Habitations.]
I. Title. II. Animal homes (Mankato, Minn.)
QL737.C22 R87 2005
599.775—dc22   2003024903

Summary: Simple text and photographs illustrate foxes and their dens.

Editorial Credits
Mari C. Schuh, editor; Linda Clavel, series designer; Enoch Peterson, production designer;
    Kelly Garvin, photo researcher; Karen Hieb, product planning editor

Photo Credits
Bruce Coleman Inc./Erwin and Peggy Bauer, 11; Hans Reinhard, cover; James Allen, 9; Jeff Foott, 6–7
Corbis/D. Robert & Lorri Franz, 12–13, 17; Lynda Richardson, 5
Corel, 1
Nature Picture Library/Andrew Cooper, 15
Tom and Pat Leeson, 18–19, 21

Note to Parents and Teachers

The Animal Homes series supports national science standards related to life
science. This book describes and illustrates foxes and their dens. The images
support early readers in understanding the text. The repetition of words and
phrases helps early readers learn new words. This book also introduces early
readers to subject-specific vocabulary words, which are defined in the Glossary.
Early readers may need assistance to read some words and to use the Table of
Contents, Glossary, Read More, Internet Sites, and Index/Word List sections
of the book.

Word Count: 146
Early-Intervention Level: 14

Table of Contents

Dens 4

Young Foxes. 14

A Good Home 20

Glossary 22

Read More 23

Internet Sites 23

Index/Word List. 24

Dens

Foxes are animals
in the dog family.
Foxes live in dens.

5

Fox dens are under
the ground, in caves,
or in hollow trees.
Foxes put leaves and
grass in their dens.

Arctic foxes make their dens in snow. They dig into the ice and snow on the ground.

Foxes sometimes use dens
made by other animals.
Foxes dig to make
the den bigger.

Fox dens often have more than one opening. Foxes can escape if a predator enters the den.

Young Foxes

Young foxes are called pups.

Pups are born in spring.

As many as 10 pups are born at one time. The pups grow fur. They stay safe and warm in the den.

Adult foxes bring food
to the den for their pups.
The pups live with their
parents for about two years.

A Good Home

Foxes use the same den
for many years. Dens
are good homes for foxes.

Glossary

cave—a large hole under the ground or in the side of a hill or cliff

escape—to get away or break free

hollow—having an empty space inside

predator—an animal that hunts and eats other animals

pup—a young fox; young foxes are also called kits.

Read More

Gibson, Deborah Chase. *Foxes and Their Homes.* Animal Habitats. New York: PowerKids Press, 1999.

Olien, Rebecca. *Foxes: Clever Hunters.* The Wild World of Animals. Mankato, Minn.: Bridgestone Books, 2002.

Swanson, Diane. *Foxes.* Welcome to the World of Animals. Milwaukee: Gareth Stevens, 2003.

Internet Sites

FactHound offers a safe, fun way to find Internet sites related to this book. All of the sites on FactHound have been researched by our staff.

Here's how:

1. Visit *www.facthound.com*

2. Type in this special code **0736825835** for age-appropriate sites. Or enter a search word related to this book for a more general search.

3. Click on the **Fetch It** button.

FactHound will fetch the best sites for you!

Index/Word List

animals, 4, 10

born, 14, 16

caves, 6

dig, 8, 10

dog, 4

escape, 12

food, 18

fur, 16

grass, 6

grow, 16

homes, 20

leaves, 6

live, 4, 18

opening, 12

parents, 18

predator, 12

pups, 14, 16, 18

safe, 16

snow, 8

spring, 14

trees, 6

warm, 16